My Soccer Diary

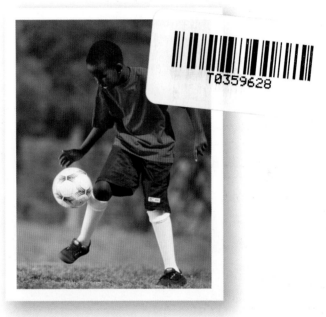

Written by Marilyn Woolley

Photography by Michael Curtain

Flying Start
to Literacy®

Contents

I wish I could play soccer

Monday, 5 April

Today was my first day at my new school. I had to figure out how to do lots of new things.

In the playground it was hard to make new friends. The games were different and I could not play them well.

I wish we could play soccer at school. I know how to play soccer.

Monday, 19 April

I asked my teacher if we could have a soccer team at school. She asked the other boys but they did not want to play soccer. They liked playing the other games better.

The teacher told me that I should try to find people to play soccer with me on the weekends.

Getting a team together

Friday, 23 April

I have asked some other boys who live near me to play soccer on Saturdays.

We needed someone to be our coach, so we asked a man who plays soccer to teach us how to play well. His name is Mike. He said he would be our coach and help us to train.

We will train at the park with Mike every week. We want to be the best soccer team and to win all our games.

Thursday, 29 April

We had training with Mike tonight for the first time. He told us we had to train hard to get fit.

We kicked the ball and we did a lot of fast running. Mike timed us and wrote down how long it took us to run 100 metres.

He told us we had to keep training so we could run faster and kick the ball well.

Thursday, 6 May

Tonight Mike showed us how to do knee jumps. I found it hard to lift my knees up to my waist.

Then Mike showed us how to kick the ball well, how to hit it with our heads and how to pass it to each other.

I practised kicking the ball past the goalkeeper and into the goal.

Our first match

Saturday, 8 May

Today we played against another team
for the first time. Before the match,
Mike told us to do our best in
every game we played.

We tried hard but we did not win.
We did not kick any goals. The other
team got two goals. I felt disappointed.

Mike was pleased that we had tried
our best. He told us that if we won
the next game he would get us all pizza.

Saturday, 15 May

Today we played a new team.

We tried to pass the ball to each other and we had two shots at the goal, but our shots did not get past the goalkeeper. The other team got three goals.

Mike told us our ball skills were getting better, but we needed to kick more goals. We did not get any pizza.

Victory at last!

Saturday, 22 May

I am so excited. We won our first game today. We played together as a team and I kicked four goals.

After the game we shook hands with the players from the other team.

Then we had pizza!

Saturday, 19 June

Now we have won five games and
I have kicked 16 goals.

Today we had our photo taken by
a photographer. A reporter asked us
about our soccer team. She is going
to write a story about our soccer team
and put it in the newspaper. She wrote
down that I had kicked the most goals.

Mike is very pleased with us. He keeps
buying us pizza.

Tuesday, 22 June

Today everyone saw our photo in the newspaper. Now the other boys at school want me to teach them how to play soccer. We will have a school soccer team soon.

The Daily Times

SOCCER TEAM WINS AGAIN!

Local soccer team, Eastside, has won its last five games. One player has kicked a remarkable 16 goals in total!

A note from the author

When we go to new places, it is often hard to learn about the different cultures and lifestyles and how to fit in and be accepted by others.

This book is based on a true story and I thought it was important to tell people about refugees' feelings and thoughts as they settle into school life in a new country. I hope this book gives the message that we should value what people are good at, rather than look for the things they cannot do.